LIFE WITH MOTHER SUPERIOR

A PLAY
BY JANE TRAHEY AND
ANNA HELEN REUTER

BASED ON JANE TRAHEY'S BOOK
LIFE WITH MOTHER SUPERIOR

★

★

DRAMATISTS
PLAY SERVICE
INC.

LIFE WITH MOTHER SUPERIOR
Copyright © Renewed 2002, Anna Helen Reuter
Copyright © 1974, Jane Trahey and Anna Helen Reuter

Based on Jane Trahey's book *Life with Mother Superior*
Copyright © Renewed 1990, Jane Trahey
Copyright © 1962, Jane Trahey

All Rights Reserved

CAUTION: Professionals and amateurs are hereby warned that performance of LIFE WITH MOTHER SUPERIOR is subject to payment of a royalty. It is fully protected under the copyright laws of the United States of America, and of all countries covered by the International Copyright Union (including the Dominion of Canada and the rest of the British Commonwealth), and of all countries covered by the Pan-American Copyright Convention, the Universal Copyright Convention, the Berne Convention, and of all countries with which the United States has reciprocal copyright relations. All rights, including without limitation professional/amateur stage rights, motion picture, recitation, lecturing, public reading, radio broadcasting, television, video or sound recording, all other forms of mechanical, electronic and digital reproduction, transmission and distribution, such as CD, DVD, the Internet, private and file-sharing networks, information storage and retrieval systems, photocopying, and the rights of translation into foreign languages are strictly reserved. Particular emphasis is placed upon the matter of readings, permission for which must be secured from the Authors' agent in writing.

The English language amateur stage performance rights in the United States, its territories, possessions and Canada for LIFE WITH MOTHER SUPERIOR are controlled exclusively by DRAMATISTS PLAY SERVICE, INC., 440 Park Avenue South, New York, NY 10016. No nonprofessional performance of the Play may be given without obtaining in advance the written permission of DRAMATISTS PLAY SERVICE, INC., and paying the requisite fee.

Inquiries concerning all other rights should be addressed to Dramatists Play Service, Inc., 440 Park Avenue South, New York, NY 10016.

SPECIAL NOTE
Anyone receiving permission to produce LIFE WITH MOTHER SUPERIOR is required to give credit to the Authors as sole and exclusive Authors of the Play on the title page of all programs distributed in connection with performances of the Play and in all instances in which the title of the Play appears for purposes of advertising, publicizing or otherwise exploiting the Play and/or a production thereof. The names of the Authors must appear on a separate line, in which no other names appear, immediately beneath the title and in size of type equal to 50% of the size of the largest, most prominent letter used for the title of the Play. No person, firm or entity may receive credit larger or more prominent than that accorded the Authors.

Act I

Bad Day for Black Sock
The Secrets of the Cloister
Days of Wrath
The Contest

Act II

September Song
The Sour Note
The Death of Abraham Lincoln
Cum Diploma

TIME: 1931 and 1935
PLACE: In and around Chicago

CAST IN ORDER OF APPEARANCE

MISS CONNELLY
GYMNASIUM GIRL I
GYMNASIUM GIRL II
GYMNASIUM GIRL III
GYMNASIUM GIRL IV
MOTHER SUPERIOR
MARY CLANCEY
WINIFRED WERTHEIM
PEGGY SCHLESSMAN
JANE MOORE
OLD LADY*
SISTER ANGELA
KATE DONAVAN
RAMONA SAPLIN
MARVEL ANN MOORE
FLORENCE MACKEY
MISS McBRIDE
MR. GOETTINGER
ROGER
GINGER
SISTER BLANCHE
MISS TOOMEY
ROGER
SISTER MARY EILLIAM
LILLIAN QUIGLEY
FRESHMAN 1
FRESHMAN 2
ANNA MARIE FLAHERTY

* Old Nun in Cloister—could be doubled. Other school girls could be used.

Life with Mother Superior

ACT I

As the curtain rises, the spot is centered and we see a high school gymnasium. Girls in old fashioned gym outfits, bloomers and middy blouses, long sleeved and floppy. It was the most modest way to play basketball. The fact that one could move at all was a miracle in itself. Long stockings were worn under the knickers along with the sneakers. No part of the body was exposed except the face. There is a group of girls exercising with dumbbells (it helps to paint them bright colors).

The girls are singing the exercise song.* At one point, a girl drops her dumbbell. Miss Connelly freezes. Miss Connelly is the gym teacher at St. Mark's. She is ranchy and efficiently bumbly. She wears a tweed skirt with a heavy, white knit cardigan that hits her right at her knee. The skirt hits her mid-calf. The school crest is sewn on the sweater. She wears a large whistle on a cord around her neck and from time to time she puts it in her mouth and forgets it is there. This provokes a rather strange speech pattern. Miss Connelly blows whistle. A spot picks up the girl who has dropped the dumbbell. She steps forward.

GIRL 1. The only difference between this school and a reformatory is tuition. My parents PAY for me to be here instead of having me committed. (*More song—another dumbell drops. All freeze.*)

GIRL 2. The rules and the food are just about the same at St. Mark's as they are at the County School for Bad Girls. (*Again exercise and another freeze. This time the girl hits Miss Connelly with her dumbbell. Miss Connelly orders her out. As she exits left, girl steps forward.*)

GIRL 3. My mother says it isn't enough to be Catholic and Irish, I have to be a lady, too. (*Back to exercise. Mother Superior enters*

* Music for this song is reproduced at end of play.

R. *Miss Connelly blows her whistle and the girls drop exhausted to the floor.*)
MOTHER SUPERIOR. Miss Connelly, I just had a call from the station master. Our four new students missed their connections and are now at the Willowood Station. Will you bring them back to school?
MISS CONNELLY. Certainly, Mother, I'll be happy to. Class—attention! March! (*Class marches out carrying dumbbells. Miss Connelly follows marching also. Mother Superior watches them and exits R. Blackout. Second curtain closes. Transition music. Lights come up. All four girls waiting D. R. Old lady sits on her suitcase. A railroad sign reads "Willowood Station." The girls study each other as strangers do. Part curiosity, part boredom. Then Mary breaks ice. Mary Clancey seems to fit her clothes better than the rest of them. She wears her school beret at a jaunty angle and reads a paperback. Winifred Wertheim is short and fat and intense. She wears glasses and looks nervous. Peggy Schlessman is tall, dark and brooding. Jane Moore is blonde. Her beret is smashed on her head.*)
MARY. (*Putting her book in her coat pocket.*) Anyone got a cigarette?
JANE. Uh, no. I smoked all mine in a state of severe depression.
MARY. Never mind, I have some *Twenty Grands*. (*Mary lights up and hands Jane one. Jane lights up and does the usual coughing reaction. You know she hasn't had much experience inhaling. An old lady watches them in disgust, blowing the smoke away with her pocketbook.*)
OLD LADY. (*Passing them by.*) You two ought to be ashamed of yourselves. Smoking at your age!
MARY. I'm not as young as you think. I am a forty-seven year old midget.
JANE. And I'm her sixty-seven year old mother!
OLD LADY. You are both candidates for the looney bin. The Sisters won't stand for this sort of thing. (*She exits R.*)
JANE. Where are you from?
MARY. California, by way of London, by way of New York.
JANE. Wow. Have you really been to all those places? What does your father do?
MARY. I haven't got a father. I live with an uncle who's in the

export business and I travel with him a lot. I have been to eleven schools so far.

JANE. Eleven schools! How marvelous! How did you end up at dreary St. Mark's?

MARY. Well, this year, Freddie—that's my uncle—had to go to the Orient. So he checked me here for the season. (*Miss Connelly enters L.*)

MISS CONNELLY. Line up, girls! Line up everyone for St. Mark's. Line up. Good afternoon, girls! I'm Miss Connelly and I'm part of the lay faculty at St. Mark's. Now if you're all lined up, we'll count heads.

MARY. Don't you think she's overdoing it a bit? There *are* only four of us!

MISS CONNELLY. When I call your names, please answer "Here!"

MARY. (*To Jane.*) Let's not answer!

JANE. Okay with me. (*To girl nearest her.*) Don't answer when she calls your name. Hear!

MARY. (*To other girls.*) Don't answer when she calls your name.

MISS CONNELLY. All right. All right. Line up. Please. Clancey! Moore. Schlessman. Wertheim. (*Turning over card to see what's wrong.*) Schlessman?

GROUP. Giggles (*All but Mary. Mary gives group withering look.*)

MISS CONNELLY. Aren't these your names?

MARY. No, Ma'am!

MISS CONNELLY. Well, then, who are you? (*Gets pencil from her bag ... it's not easy.*) All right now, spell out your names, one at a time.

MARY. F–A–Y.

MISS CONNELLY. First or last name?

MARY. First!

MISS CONNELLY. Last?

MARY. Wray, W–R–A–Y.

MISS CONNELLY. (*Pointing to Jane.*) Next!

JANE. My name is Pawnee and I'm a full-blooded Seminole.

MISS CONNELLY. You are? Oh dear, Mother Superior must have given me the wrong list to meet. Well, no matter, we're glad you're here nevertheless. Come on, I'll get the rest of your names later and we'll straighten the whole thing out when we get to St. Mark's. Let's get some exercise on our way. (*She blows whistle on whole scene and begins to jog. Girls follow, but only after she makes them. Girls jog to* D. R. *then up to* U. R.—*across to* U. L. *and end* D. R. *A strobe light following them would be effective. They are now outside St. Mark's. The wall and chute are presumably in the audience area. A curtain closes behind the group.*) There we are, girls. Welcome to St. Mark's. Isn't it beautiful?

MARY. It looks like something right out of King Arthur.

JANE. Look at that wall, will you? I'll bet it's nine feet high!

WERTHEIM. What's that funny thing, Miss Connelly?

MISS CONNELLY. That's our fire escape. It's a kind of chute like they have on playgrounds, only it's all enclosed.

MARY. Do we get to use it?

MISS CONNELLY. Oh yes, every time we have a fire drill. There's an outlet on every floor. Now, wait here girls, while I find Mother. I don't know how I came by this list of wrong names. (*Exits* R. *She leaves jogging.* R.)

SCHLESSMAN. I don't think we should go on lying.

WERTHEIM. I don't either. After all . . .

MARY. (*Pointing to Schlessman.*) Your first name is Ada and you pronounce it Adda. OK? And you (*Pointing to Wertheim.*) your name is Bottom, Sandy Bottom. (*From* R. *Mother Superior enters. Miss Connelly follows her jogging. The kids watch cautiously. Mother Superior is tall, dark, and as medieval looking as the place itself. She is the high lama of her monastery. She keeps her arms folded under her cape. Schlessman giggles nervously. Mother Superior glances at her and if a glance could kill, there would be no more Schlessman.*)

MISS CONNELLY. (*Whistling.*) Attention, girls. Here is Mother Superior. Mother, here are four lovely, new freshmen.

MOTHER SUPERIOR. (*Coldly as possible.*) How do you do.

MISS CONNELLY. Mother, there seems to have been a mix-up. I was supposed to have picked up these four (*She points at her list.*) but I got these four. (*She turns over card.*) I got Wray, Bottom, Lemmon and Pawnee. (*Fascinated.*) Did you know she is a pure bred Seminole?

MOTHER SUPERIOR. Truly? I had no idea we had any pure breeds in this class. Which one of you is Pawnee?

JANE. I am. Me. I am Pawnee!
MOTHER SUPERIOR. And what is you first name, Pawnee.
JANE. (*Determined not to be caught.*) Black Sock.
MOTHER SUPERIOR. Black Sock? And who is Miss Wray? What is Miss Wray's first name, Miss Connelly? Don't tell me it's Fay? (*Miss Connelly shakes her head in wonderment at Mother Superior's super intuitiveness.*)
MARY. Yes, it's Fay. Fay W-R-A-Y!
MOTHER SUPERIOR. I am quite capable of spelling the name Fay and Wray. And who is Miss Bottom?
WERTHEIM. I am.
JANE. Her first name is Sandra, but everyone calls her "Sandy."
MOTHER SUPERIOR. If Miss Bottom had enough brains to get to high school, I must assume she can remember her first name WITHOUT HELP. (*To Schlessman.*) I must then assume that you are Miss Lemmon. It would be too much to expect your first name is "Sour."
WERTHEIM. Oh Mother, my name isn't Bottom, it's Wertheim. Winifred Wertheim. And she's Peggy Schlessman. Everyone calls me Wendy.
MOTHER SUPERIOR. (*Having had it.*) I do not care ONE whit what everyone calls anyone. I am interested in getting just one thing. The simple truth. Just your real names would do in this particular instance. Miss Wertheim and Miss Schlessman may go with Miss Connelly. Write a two page letter of apology to Miss Connelly for lying to her. Miss Wray and our pure breed can stay here for a moment. (*Miss Connelly is obviously undone. She takes the two girls out R. and as they leave they both try to explain to her that it wasn't their fault.*) I suppose you are Miss Clancey, or is it you?
MARY. It's me.
MOTHER SUPERIOR. The answer to that question is "Yes, Mother." And you are Adrienne Moore?
JANE. (*Truly looking pained.*) Well, no. I'm Jane. Jane Moore.
MOTHER SUPERIOR. You will say, "No, Mother," if you please.
JANE. (*Sheepishly.*) No, Mother.
MOTHER SUPERIOR. Your name is NOT Adrienne? How many pseudonyms do you have? Your record says your name is Adrienne.
JANE. I know. I made Adrienne up. I thought it had more distinc-

tion, more mystery than just plain Jane, so I wrote it on my graduation form.

MOTHER SUPERIOR. You lied to the authorities about your name at graduation?

JANE. (*Laughing.*) My father almost fell off his chair.

MOTHER SUPERIOR. That is quite enough. Now you two, listen. There is to be no lying here at St. Mark's. And no games. Do you understand me?

PAIR. *Yes*, Mother.

MOTHER SUPERIOR. Dismissed. I hope we never meet again under such circumstances. Go right to your rooms. You may go to chapel (*She points to Mary.*) and you may skip dinner. I'm sure you have no appetite now. (*Mary and Jane exit hurriedly R. Mary forgets her tennis racquet and Mother Superior picks it up and calls after her. She then tosses an imaginary ball into the air and socks it down court. Sister Angela comes in L. spies her and gives her a fast net return. Sister Angela is medium height, fairly young, peppy, snarky, and funny.*)

SISTER ANGELA. Helen Wills Moody, I presume. A beautiful service. (*They play a few serves—back and forth.*)

MOTHER SUPERIOR. Heavens, that's enough. If I tried to play a whole set these days, I'd be in line for the pulmotor.

SISTER ANGELA. I hear we have a brand new shipment of fresh eggs.

MOTHER SUPERIOR. You heard right. Let me tell you.

SISTER ANGELA. Don't. I've had it all from Miss Connelly. If this is first day material, spare me from the second semester.

MOTHER SUPERIOR. You won't have any trouble from Schlessman and Wertheim, but I have a sneaky suspicion that this is only the beginning for Black Sock and Fay Wray.

SISTER ANGELA. I thought her name was Pawnee.

MOTHER SUPERIOR. (*Laughing.*) Pawnee, my dear, is her tribal name. However, family can call her Black Sock.

SISTER ANGELA. (*Imitating Miss Connelly with whistle.*) Is she really a full bred Seminole?

MOTHER SUPERIOR. She's a full bred Irishman. Poor Helen Connelly. She's a dear, but so naïve.

SISTER ANGELA. Well, she swallows just about anything, but I pray she hangs on to her whistle. (*Bell rings.*)

MOTHER SUPERIOR. Oh, oh. Do me a favor, old dear. See that Fay Wray gets her golf clubs and her sports gear and her tennis racquet (*She picks up all the stuff.*) and Angela, remind me that when we do class lists, we split that team right down the middle. Get the word out. (*Mother Superior exits. Angela exits L. During the scene between the two sisters played D. C. Faculty and students could bring in stools and place them in a semi-circle U. C. behind curtain. Curtain opens and lights come up on all the girls singing school song.* A nun is conducting as only a serious nun music teacher can conduct. Near the conclusion of the song, Mother Superior enters and stands U. C.*) I think one of the first things we must learn is our school song. Now, I have one very important announcement. It's a cardinal rule here at St. Mark's. You are not, as you well know, the only people who live here. We (*She points to the faculty.*) live here. And there is a part of the building that is reserved EXCLUSIVELY—EX-CLU-SIVE-LY for us. It is forbidden to enter, under any circumstances, any section of the cloister. It is clearly marked on all doors. I must assume that you all read and if you can't, please have someone point out the letters so you will recognize them as taboo.
MARY. (*Leaning over Jane.*) Sarcasm. Sarcasm. The devil's own weapon!
MOTHER SUPERIOR. Miss Clancey. Is your message so important that you talk while I am trying to talk?
MARY. I'm sorry Mother, I thought that Miss Moore was going to faint and I asked her if she felt all right. (*Jane looks at Mary dumbfounded. She wiggles in her seat, uncomfortable. Mary pats her on the shoulder, sits down and meekly folds her hands in her lap.*)
MOTHER SUPERIOR. Well, hold on, Miss Moore. Just another minute and you can have the floor to yourself. Now the cloister is OUR home. We don't want strangers roaming around it. If I find anyone of you in the Cloister at any time, you will have only me to answer to. Is that clear?
STUDENTS. Yes, Mother.
MOTHER SUPERIOR. Good. We're planning a very special welcome dinner this evening since this is the feast day of our order. I hope you will enjoy it and your stay at St. Mark's. You may now

* Lyrics for this song are reproduced at end of play.

go directly to the Dining Hall. (*The girls start to leave* L.) Oh, Miss Moore. Since you feel faint, you had better skip dinner and see Sister Nurse.
JANE. Oh, I feel just fine now. It was just a case of my severe claustrophobia.
MOTHER SUPERIOR. Ah . . . another fascinating facet of your personality emerges. See Sister Nurse NOW.
JANE. Couldn't I see her after dinner?
MOTHER SUPERIOR. Now! (*Mother Superior exits* R. *Blackout. Curtain closes. Lights up on a small area at* R. *Jane sits dejectedly alone waiting. Mary enters with Kate Donavan, another student. She's cute looking and sharp. Mary has a very fat bosom now and extracts two oranges from it and a roll.*)
JANE. Where have you been? I'm starved.
MARY. I got here as soon as I could. And I've brought us a partner for our new project. This is Kate Donavan.
JANE. These oranges are red hot.
MARY. What did you expect . . . they're bosom temperature. They've been next to me since dinner began.
JANE. This is it . . . dinner?
MARY. Eat your roll first. The oranges will cool off.
JANE. It has no butter or anything on it.
MARY. Oh, stop complaining.
JANE. Complaining? Me? Complaining? Why shouldn't I? I'm the one who gets to skip all the meals. You do everything you want to do and you get to eat. It's not fair. Do you know I have not had one meal since we arrived?
MARY. I'll get you something later when Mother Superior goes into her forbidden cloister. (*She makes it sound mysterious.*)
JANE. I ought to get my father a discount on food.
MARY. Oh come on, forget it. I have had a simply smashing idea. Utterly deeeeee-vine. I want the three of us to go in the tour business.
JANE. TOUR BUSINESS? Touring what?
MARY. We are going to tour the cloister!
KATE. Forget it. I'm not going to get expelled. And that's what that monster has in mind if we get caught. Count me out.
MARY. We are not going to get caught.
JANE. Kate's right. It's just too risky.

MARY. It's not risky at all. It's kid stuff. I spent a whole hour in it and I didn't get caught.
JANE. YOU HAVE BEEN IN THERE ALREADY?
MARY. It's a snap. First of all, everyone goes to prayers at four-thirty, *including* Mother Superior. They stay there exactly one hour and twenty-one minutes. You could tour Versailles in that length of time.
KATE. What about the nun at the front door?
MARY. She sleeps all the time. She's over a thousand years old.
JANE. How do you get in?
MARY. By the gym. There's a door that leads right into their visiting rooms. From there we can go into the dining room and up a flight to the bedrooms. We never go near the chapel and that's where they all are.
JANE. But we need a lookout.
MARY. We can take turns. Kate will be lookout one day. You another, and I'll tour the group.
KATE. I say forget it. I'm not going near the place.
MARY. Then you can be permanent lookout. Right, Pawnee? (*Pawnee looks convinced.*) We'll take the groups through and you'll still get your third of the take.
JANE. You're going to charge for the tour?
MARY. Of course. I figure every kid in this place is worth a quarter.
JANE. You're insane. You can't take everyone. Someone is bound to talk.
MARY. No one dares open their mouths. They'll be afraid. Those that have done it are in trouble and those who haven't will want desperately to do it. We can't lose. It's got a built in glamor. We'll call it the *Medieval Torture Tour of the Cloister.*
KATE. I don't know. It still doesn't seem worth the risks.
MARY. Look, give me one other way to make one hundred and fifty thousand dollars.
KATE. It's a hundred and fifty dollars if we got every kid in the place.
JANE. We'll get 'em.
KATE. OK. On one condition. If I so much as smell the enemy, I'm cutting. I'll try and signal if I can. But I won't take any chances. (*Blackout—transition music. Lights up on another area of*

stage, D. R. *Conversation between Schlessman, Marvel Ann, Saplin, Mackey, Quigley, and Wertheim until Mary enters and shushes them.*)
MARY. OK everybody! Ready? Today's the day for your very own special exclusive tour of the Cloister of St. Mark's. It's a very good day as we've had word that a real flagellant is loose.
GROUP. Ohhhh. What's a flagellant?
MARY. It's someone who whips himself because he's so holy.
RAMONA SAPLIN. This is ridiculous. I want my money back.
MARY. Sorry. You held a reservation for today. Now you pay whether you go or not.
JANE. Where's Kate? We better wait till she gets here.
MARY. (*Taking Jane aside.*) She couldn't make it today. She had to go to the dentist.
JANE. Then I don't think we should take a chance.
MARY. Don't be ridiculous. We haven't seen a soul in ten days of touring. And we get to split this money 50-50. (*Without Kate.*)
JANE. Yeah . . . that's right. (*Always willing to get her cut.*) If you straggle, we cannot be responsible for you or your safety. We have heard that captive girls are often sold to mission countries and their parents never hear of them again.
GROUP. How awful. Let's be careful. Watch out.
MARVEL ANN. Who told you that pack of lies?
JANE. No one told me. I just know it's true. (*The group moves across the stage to* R. *Curtain opens. We are now in the cloister.*) Now pay attention. (*Pointing to audience area* D. L.) Here on the left is the refectory. That's what religious call their dining room. As you can see by its cheerless decor, you wouldn't have any appetite here anyway.
MARY. The skull and crossbones on the wall are a symbol for the cuisine served in St. Mark's. (*As the group moves on, they are shadowed by Mother Superior, who keeps just far enough behind to stay out of their vision, but quite in view of the audience.*)
JANE. The lectern is where one of the nuns reads psalms or highly spiritual books. You know that nuns do not talk to each other at meals. That's probably just as well. Now on to the bedrooms.
MARVEL ANN. (*Tugging at Mary's sleeve.*) Is that all there is on this floor? (*They all move* U. R. *and to* L. *and then* D. *to* D. R.)
MARY. What did you expect, corpses of ancient priests?

JANE. Come on!

RAMONA. Well, I for one agree with Marvel. For twenty-five cents just seeing a dining room is a gyp.

JANE. If you don't like it, just leave now and find your own way back. No one is holding you. (*The bedrooms are off* R.)

MARY. (*Trying to get a group spirit going, turns on charm.*) Now here's a typical convent dormitory. At night, these curtains are pulled around each bed to insure privacy. Not a sound is made here after solemn silence.

JANE. (*To Mary.*) Listen, I hear someone coming. Duck. Get in the closet. (*The group panics and scatters in fear. A nun in bathrobe and cap comes across stage and reads the morning paper the whole time.*)

MARY. (*Quick to take advantage.*) Now. Now. See. That was an authentic species of a nun wearing a tribal nighttime outfit of the order. (*On this cue, Mother Superior stuffs her handkerchief in her mouth.*)

JANE. OK. Let's go.

FLORENCE. Go? Where are the torture instruments you promised . . . the whip they beat novices with during Lent? (*Mother Superior exits* U. L. *Door locks off.*)

MARY. If they're not locked away in Mother Superior's quarters, you'll see them soon enough. Now here is the highlight of the tour. Mother Superior's very own room.

JANE. (*Takes robe from off* R. *bedroom.*) Here is a prime example of a hair shirt (*She drops it like a hot cake and winces from the pain.*) It is worn for self-effacement and punishment. Most you've read about are just shirts, but Mother Superior's is a full length robe, so she must be in deep trouble.

RAMONA. (*Gingerly touching it.*) Oh you con artist! It's nothing but flannel. You two are a pack of liars!

JANE. (*Picks up robe with a one finger.*) You are crazy, Ramona. You have no feeling. Here, Schlessman, you feel. (*Schlessman feels and screams. That's just what Jane wanted. She gives Ramona a disgusted look and the group now seems totally satisfied.*)

MARY. Now this officially ends the tour. We exit here. Turn left when you get inside the door and open the next one just beyond it. You'll be right back in the gym. From there on you can find your

own way back, but don't go in groups. One at a time. Please. (*Group goes first. Florence tries pushing door off* L. *that Mother Superior has already locked. Nothing happens.*)
FLORENCE. (*Turning to group in panic.*) The door is locked. It won't open. (*Group starts to scream. Mary runs to front and tries. Ramona faints.*)
JANE. (*Coming up to front.*) Oh for heaven's sake! Give it a shove. (*She shoves. Nothing happens.*) OK. We'll switch plans. Don't panic. We'll use the bedroom door and this will bring us out by the . . . the chemistry lab. OK, let's go. Come on, get Ramona up. (*Mary tries this door at* R. *Nothing happens.*)
FLORENCE. Listen you two. If I don't get out of here, I'll lose my honor ribbons.
MARY. (*To Jane.*) If they get caught, it's honor ribbons. If we get caught, it's heads. Come on, we're ditching them. (*Mary and Jane start running down front stage. Group pulls Ramona off stage and lights follow Mary and Jane.*)
JANE. Who do you think locked all the doors?
MARY. Who do you think?
JANE. That's what I thought. Well, what'll we do?
MARY. We're going to get out. Listen, I have just had theeeeee most deeeeeeee-vine idea. Let's use the fire escape.
JANE. But we're on the fourth floor!
MARY. Sit down and I'll give you a shove. (*Scream from Jane as she is pushed down. They exit* L. *Blackout. Curtain opens. Chute has been moved in* U. L. *Lights pick up girls coming down chute.*)
JANE. What luck! Boy that was close.
MARY. Just wait till Mother Superior finds Ramona and Marvel Ann. (*She simply chuckles with glee.*)
JANE. Let's get out of here. I've had it for today. I need a cigarette desperately! (*As they get up to leave, brushing their uniforms, the light widens and there stands Mother Superior.*)
MOTHER SUPERIOR. (*Beckoning them to follow her.*) As they say, "Where there's smoke, there's fire." (*Blackout—curtain closes. Chute is moved off. Sewing room is set up at* U. R. *Art room is set up at* U. L. *Mother Superior walks them across stage to another spot.* D. R. *There are buckets and scrub brushes. She points to them them and exits,* R. *Jane and Mary start scrubbing and sing the song,*

"Life with Mother Superior."* At conclusion of song, girls have scrubbed their way off, R. During this song, Sister Angela sets up her "Studio" U. R. It consists of a large easel with a canvas. She starts slapping paint on a huge canvas. She wears a huge apron of black and white stripes and she has removed her sleeves. She keeps one brush between her teeth and changes it from time to time. Mother Superior comes briskly onto the stage and gives Sister Angela's painting a look and nods with pleasure.) Ah, Angela dear! I was hoping I would find you. (She peers at painting.) My, that is effective!

SISTER ANGELA. Wherever you use words like "effective," I know you hate it, but you need a favor.

MOTHER SUPERIOR. Why Angela, no such thing.

SISTER ANGELA. I know you want to dump one of those terrors on me at three every afternoon.

MOTHER SUPERIOR. Wherever did you hear that?

SISTER ANGELA. There is no such thing as a secret in this place.

MOTHER SUPERIOR. OK. You're right. I have them doing every chore in the place.

SISTER ANGELA. If they keep up their performance, we can fire one of the janitors.

MOTHER SUPERIOR. It's no way for them to get an education. I think it's time we took a new tack. Split them up completely and get them into different interest areas. Moore is going to learn to sew in the late afternoon class and Mary—well, I thought Mary might hit it off with you in sculpture. She has shown some interest in some of our own statuary.

SISTER ANGELA. She's probably trying to figure out a way for St. Joseph to hit you as you cross the front hall.

MOTHER SUPERIOR. Oh Angela. She can't be all bad. She likes sculpting.

SISTER ANGELA. If she's interested in sculpting, it's because there is a certain amount of chiseling involved. *She is evil!*

MOTHER SUPERIOR. Honestly, you a teacher. The problem is she's bored. She's had a very exciting life gallivanting with her mad uncle across five continents, then she ends up here and all she can think of is pranks to keep her awake. In a way, I understand her.

* Music for this song is reproduced at end of play.

SISTER ANGELA. How can you be so naïve? You've got them booked solid and they still find time at midnight to prowl through the laundry room and sew up every sister's nightgown. *And* with the back stitch!
MOTHER SUPERIOR. Oh come on. Give her a chance. Look, I'll make a deal. If she gets out of line just let me know and I'll send her home. After all, there is just so much *we* have to take.
SISTER ANGELA. *We* don't have to take anything. If she gets out of line in my vision, you won't have to send her home. Try a hospital.
MOTHER SUPERIOR. That's the easy way out. Sure she's wild, but it's the wild ones that make interesting people.
SISTER ANGELA. You're right. There are hundreds of fascinating people behind bars this very moment. (*Mother Superior looks sad. Sister Angela gives a final dash to her work.*) OK, I'll try. But you tell her that I don't play games.
MOTHER SUPERIOR. You are a doll! (*She exits.*)
SISTER ANGELA. I knew my luck wouldn't hold up. (*Lights dim on Sister Angela as she continues to paint. Lights come up on Mary and Jane D. R. again, on their knees scrubbing. Mother Superior enters. Stops at Mary's pail, front R., and surveys job. She rubs her fingers along the top of a chair, or whatever stage prop is handy.*)
MOTHER SUPERIOR. When you finish in this area, you can move over to the cloister door area. Since you are so fond of this part of the building, I know you'll want to participate in the maintenance of it. Shine the doorknobs, but do not turn the doorknobs. Do you understand?
MARY. (*Leaning back on her heels.*) You'd have to let me in if I joined the convent.
MOTHER SUPERIOR. The day you come in, I go out. Now when you are through for the day you can report to Sister Angela. She's expecting you at three. (*Mary gets up and rubs her knees. Mother Superior crosses to where Jane is scrubbing.*) All right, Jane. Get up. Put your things away. I'm taking you to meet Miss McBride.
JANE. (*Struggling to get up.*) Just a minute, Mother, I am kneeling on a hangnail.
MOTHER SUPERIOR. Just pick it up and tuck it in. I want every shred of your effort for this next project. Come on. (*Mother

Superior and Jane cross over to L. *As they do, lights come up on group including Ramona, Wertheim, Schlessman and Marvel Ann, all sitting in chairs around a table. Miss McBride enters from other side, bows to Mother Superior. Miss McBride is dressed in a 3 piece grey knit suit. She wears gold scissors on a string around her neck. She has a pin cushion tied on her wrist. Mother Superior hands over her charge like a warden with a prisoner to new warden. Miss McBride hands Jane a shopping bag and points out a place for her to sit. Mother Superior and Miss McBride nod formally and Mother Superior exits. Miss McBride, like a conductor, raises the class to their feet.*)

MISS McBRIDE. (*Crossing her arms on her chest, bows her head.*) Dear Lord, help uth to utilithe well each and evewy moment thpent here. (*She signals them to sit.*) Thith morning we begin our thpethial project clath. I hope thith clath will be moth rewarding. Now the firth letthon we muth learn is what evewy artithan learnth—the care of oneth toolths. You muth take good care of your toolths. Your thissorth and needleth and pinth. (*She signals to take everything out of the bag. Jane takes her bag and turns it upside down and the scissors fall out on Ramona's foot.*)

RAMONA. (*Screaming.*) Oh, LOOK what you've done! My foot it bleeding.

MISS McBRIDE. (*Running to Ramona, who now falls into a dead faint.*) Oh dear Lordth!

JANE. (*Bored.*) There she goes again!

MISS McBRIDE. Now, juth thee what you have done. Poor Ramona. Someone go get Thithter Nurth.

JANE. (*Propping up Ramona.*) She'll be OK. Just get her head between her legs. (*Ramona does not like this and sits up on her own. Miss McBride helps her to her feet.*)

MISS McBRIDE. Marvel Ann, take Ramona to Thithter Nurth.

JANE. I'll take her. I stabbed her.

MISS McBRIDE. (*Furious.*) You have done enough. Thit down thisth inthanth! (*Ramona and Marvel Ann exit R.*) Now where were we. Oh yeth, we are going to make a lovely pair of thilk pantieth from Butterick Pattern Company number theven nine thikth.

JANE. (*Disgusted.*) Is it possible to make something else? I wouldn't wear orange silk panties if I died. I want to make a Ginger Rogers outfit.

MISS McBRIDE. No! No! No! No Ginger Rogerth outfitth in thith clath.

CLASS. Oh Miss McBride. Let's make culottes. Shorts. Carole Lombard dresses.

MISS McBRIDE. Huth up, girlth. What would Mother Thuperior thay. No, we muth make our thilk troutheau. Pantieth belong in a ladieth troutheau. *And that ith what we are going to make.*

JANE. But we won't ever wear them.

MISS McBRIDE. Nevertheleth, you are going to make them. If you don't like it, tell Mother Thuperior.

JANE. I'll make them.

MISS McBRIDE. Now, for every pair there are two parths. Front and back.

SCHLESSMAN. *(Holding up her pattern.)* I've got three pieces, Miss McBride.

MISS McBRIDE. *(Putting her head in her hands.)* Pleath, for my thake, put that part away. We come to that tomorrow. Now take out your peach thilk and thpwead it out carefully. *(Lights dim on sewing class and come up on Sister Angela [far R.] who is painting busily. Mary comes in behind her and peers around. She studies the painting and shakes her head. She pokes around until Sister Angela spies her and grabs her in a karate hold.)*

SISTER ANGELA. An idle mind is a devil's workshop. What do you think you are doing here?

MARY. I'm supposed to be in a sculpture class.

SISTER ANGELA. You are in a sculpture class.

MARY. Where is everybody?

SISTER ANGELA. *Everybody* is here. This class is just you and me!

MARY. How jolly.

SISTER ANGELA. Don't think for one minute I want to be here any more than you do.

MARY. It wasn't my idea.

SISTER ANGELA. Just grin and bear it like I do. Give me a dollar for supplies.

MARY. I thought the supplies were paid for.

SISTER ANGELA. They are. This money is for the missions. If

I'm willing to sacrifice my time, you must sacrifice your money. GIVE!
MARY. (*Backing off, knocks over the painting of Sister Angela's.*) Oh, oh!
SISTER ANGELA. (*Grabbing Mary by the neck.*) Look, if you want to break something, try your head.
MARY. (*Picking it up.*) I'm sorry. Honestly. (*Studies picture.*) It's not bad.
SISTER ANGELA. (*Flattered despite herself.*) Oh, forget it! Just be careful. Come on. Let's mix up some plaster. Do you know anything about clay?
MARY. Men have feet of it.
SISTER ANGELA. A regular poet aren't you? What do you want to make?
MARY. A huge eagle with a wingspread this wide (*She opens her arms to show spread.*) with big, bulging eyes holding a wiggling rodent in its mouth . . . something personal for Mother Superior.
SISTER ANGELA. How would you feel about a little robin?
MARY. Love it.
SISTER ANGELA. (*Working up the clay.*) Good. And what have you learned today? (*She dumps the clay in Mary's hands.*)
MARY. Idle mind. Devil's workshop.
SISTER ANGELA. I think you've got it. (*Lights dim on Angela and Mary and come up on sewing class. Miss McBride is holding up a pair of silk panties.*)
MISS McBRIDE. Oh Ramona. They're a joy. Look girlth, Ramona hath finithed her pantieth. The firth to finith. A round of applauth for Ramona. (*A few scattered claps. Jane ignores the whole scene and keeps sewing away madly.*)
WINIFRED. (*Biting off thread with her teeth.*) I'm finished too.
MISS McBRIDE. Oh, girlth, another winner! Winifred hath finithed her pantieth too. Good for Winifred. (*Miss McBride walks in and out helping and encouraging. When she comes to Jane's, she makes a face and picks up the grey, hideous mess. The lace hangs off the waist and the legs are two different lengths.*) Mith Moore. The lathe doth not go around the waitht. It goeth around the legth. Here, you muth rip it all off. (*Class giggles, Jane is furious.*) Inthidentally, girlth, I have thum interethting newth. Womenth Home Companion ith holding a contetht for original de-

signs. Firth prithe ith one hundred dollarth. Thecond prithe ith fifty dollarth. Ten runner-upth—ten dollarth and Coath and Clark will thend a thpool of evewy contheivable color they make. AND a pair of pinking shearths from THWITH Company. I have the formth on my dethk for anyone intertheted. (*Bell rings, everyone grabs their stuff and shoves it into shopping bags. Jane stands up and realizes she has sewn the panties on to her uniform.*) Mith Moore, juth look at you. You have thewn your pantieth onto your thkirt. Oh dear.
JANE. Just leave me and my pantieth alone.
MISS McBRIDE. All right, class dismissed. (*Class is delighted at Jane's dilemma. Jane rips off the panties furious at the whole thing, storms up to Miss McBride' desk and takes several forms.*) Oh dear, Mith Moore, I hope you aren't going to thend in thoth pantieth ath a joke.
JANE. I am going to design something and win that contest, (*Exiting.*) if it is the very last thing I ever do. (*Lights dim on Miss McBride. Jane crosses over to art platform, where Mary is cutting clay with a butcher knife. Lights come up on them.*)
MARY. Come on in. No one is here.
JANE. You can't be too careful. Not with HER. Do you know I was black and blue after that last go round with her.
MARY. It was your own fault. I told you not to eat her still life.
JANE. Oh, for Pete's sake. The bananas were turning black. She didn't have to throw the bowl at me.
MARY. You're lucky she didn't throw the book at you. Look at my cherub.
JANE. I thought you were making a Baby Jesus.
MARY. (*Pointing to the mess.*) She wouldn't let me call it that. She said I could call it a gorilla, or a gargoyle, but not Baby Jesus. Actually, she's kind of an original in her own way.
JANE. She scares me to death. You're sure you're not going to get in trouble staying here while she's out?
MARY. She has gone for the day. Checked out. And . . . I have theeee most MARVELOUS idea. It's absolutely deeeeee-vine. Where is Marvel Ann?
JANE. She's on her way. I told her you were going to paint her.
MARY. I've changed my mind. What I want to do is much more interesting. I'm going to make a mask of her.

JANE. Are you sure you know how?
MARY. Of course. It's no different than what I've done here.
JANE. Yes, but look at it.
MARY. Stop worrying. There wasn't a pope or a king that didn't have a face mask made.
JANE. Yeah, but they were dead when they made them. Marvel is alive.
MARY. I tell you it's OK. Angela has been coaching me. I've made four already.
JANE. But not *on* anyone. (*Marvel Ann comes in. She has an old sweater on over her uniform.*)
MARY. Come on in Marvel. I'm just about ready for you. This is going to be a sensation. (*Mary lifts her hands out of a pail. They are covered with white gook. Marvel Ann stares in horror at her.*)
MARVEL ANN. I thought you were going to paint me.
MARY. No, I'm going to sculpt you. Imagine having a head of yourself—isn't that marvelous?
MARVEL ANN. I don't want one.
MARY. Oh come on Marv. Let me try. You've got a perfect profile for one. (*Marvel Ann backs away in horror as Mary comes near her with the gook.*)
MARVEL ANN. Don't you dare put that stuff on me.
JANE. Marvel Ann, you promised you'd pose for Mary.
MARY. You can give the mask to your mother for Christmas. That will save you money and she'll love it.
MARVEL ANN. What if that stuff gets in my eyes.
MARY. It won't get in your eyes if you keep them closed. Here, sit down.
JANE. Yes, sit here. I'll stand right by and see that everything is OK. Here, put this around you. (*She picks up Sister Angela's work apron and wraps it barber style around Marvel Ann.*)
MARVEL ANN. How will I breathe?
MARY. (*Taking straws out of her pocket.*) With these in your nose. Just like underwater divers. Here, give me the oil to protect your skin. Quick.
MARVEL ANN. That's lard. My God what are you going to do, cook me? I'm leaving. You are both totally insane.
MARY. It takes ten minutes. (*Jane hold Marvel Ann down and Mary begins to slap the stuff on. They work feverishly with their*

23

backs to the audience. When they lean back, Marvel Ann's face is a huge white plastic mask.) [A dummy plastic mask could be used.] There, done. It's beautiful. If it works, I'll do a bust of you.

MARVEL ANN. (*Thrashing and moaning and crying.*) I can't breathe.

MARY. (*Adjusting straws in nose.*) There, that's better.

JANE. Can't you take it off now, it's been over 10 minutes.

MARY. (*Testing it.*) Yes, it's getting hard now.

JANE. Come on, let's get it off.

MARY. Chisel, please. (*Jane hands Mary chisel. Mary bangs away. Nothing happens.*)

JANE. Nothing's happening.

MARY. It all comes off in one piece. Hold still Marvel. Just another second.

JANE. (*Pulling on it, while holding Marvel Ann to chair with her knee. They both pull and tug and nothing happens. Marvel Ann, sensing that all is not well, screams in muffled sounds. As the pair work on, Sister Angela enters and stares in horror.*)

SISTER ANGELA. Dear Mother of God! What are you doing?

MARY. (*Trying to be casual.*) Just making a mask of Marvel Ann.

MARVEL ANN. Help, Help.

SISTER ANGELA. (*Running to Marvel Ann.*) Marvel, listen. It's me, Sister Angela. You'll be all right. Stop screaming now. I'm going to help. Go get Sister Nurse. Now Marvel, I'll have it off in a minute. (*Mary and Jane exit running. Lights dim on Marvel Ann and Sister Angela. Lights come up in sewing room. Jane is alone working on a plaid dress. Mary enters and falls to the floor.*)

MARY. I am dead! Dead! Dead! I just finished HER thousand chores for the day.

JANE. You get no sympathy from me. She worked me for six hours this week. Do you know I cleaned every paint jar this school has ever had.

MARY. I scrubbed the art floor. I removed all "those tiny ink stains that accumulate over the years" (*She imitates Sister Angela.*) I cleaned every brush she's ever owned with turp.

JANE. You have only yourself to blame. Poor Marvel. She still has sores and white specks everywhere.

MARY. I still think it would have worked if Angela had let it harden properly. It would have come off.

JANE. Yes, along with Marvel's skin.
MARY. Come on, let's go. I've had it here.
JANE. Nope. I've got to finish this.
MARY. What is that anyway? It's ugly.
JANE. It is not. It's my entry in the sewing contest. I'm going to win and with the money I'm leaving this place and no one will ever catch me.
MARY. If that wins, it will be a new era in fashion. (*She exits. Jane keeps sewing. Mother Superior comes in and not seeing Jane, turns out the lights.*)
JANE. Hey, I'm in here.
MOTHER SUPERIOR. For heaven's sake. What are you doing, hiding in here?
JANE. (*Peeved.*) I'm not hiding. I'm creating.
MOTHER SUPERIOR. I've never known you to be so involved that you missed a meal.
JANE. I don't have all that many opportunities to skip them when I want to.
MOTHER SUPERIOR. Don't blame me.
JANE. Food isn't important if you feel creative.
MOTHER SUPERIOR. Let me see what you're making.
JANE. (*Proudly.*) Here. Here it is.
MOTHER SUPERIOR. (*Puzzled.*) What is it, Jane?
JANE. It's my entry for the Butterick contest on creative design.
MOTHER SUPERIOR. How did you manage to do it?
JANE. (*Getting irritated.*) Do what?
MOTHER SUPERIOR. Cut it so badly.
JANE. I didn't cut it badly. I was careful.
MOTHER SUPERIOR (*Looking at it, and the pattern.*) Did anyone tell you that you can't cut a plaid like you do a plain fabric?
JANE. (*Near tears.*) No, we never had a plaid before. I thought it looked funny, but then I thought creative things should. All the colors go different.
MOTHER SUPERIOR. They sure do. I don't think this has a chance.
JANE. Well, damn.
MOTHER SUPERIOR. That kind of language isn't going to make it any better.
JANE. Well, it's disappointing.

MOTHER SUPERIOR. *(Inspecting it carefully.)* I think you could salvage some of it. Do you have any extra fabric?
JANE. *(Unrolling a bolt.)* Lots! I bought it for an emergency.
MOTHER SUPERIOR. *(Giving her the dress.)* You start ripping. I'll start cutting. Here, you thread a needle for me, I can't see in this light.
JANE. I had no idea you could sew.
MOTHER SUPERIOR. There are a lot of things you don't know. Here, be careful what you're doing there. We need the skirt. And for heaven's sake—what am I supposed to do with this? *(She holds up the thread Jane has given her and it is about nine feet long.)* No wonder you can't get it right. It would take you a year to do the hem with this. *(Expertly she bites off the thread.)*
JANE. I'm sorry Mother. It's just that my eyes are tired.
MOTHER SUPERIOR. Why don't you go to bed. I'll fool around with this in my room and see if I get anywhere. It may be hopeless.
JANE. You're sure you don't mind?
MOTHER SUPERIOR. No, no. It will be like old times in Paris, where I worked for the great Madame Chanel.
JANE. When you . . . worked . . . you . . .
MOTHER SUPERIOR. Go to bed, Jane. *(Jane exits. Lights fade slowly and Mother Superior, giggles happily as she exits. Music—lights up for sewing class.)*
MISS McBRIDE. Oh girlth, I am thrilled. I have invited Mother Thuperior to come and hear the good newth. THREE of our girlth entered the Womenth Home Companion Contetht and Mith Moore, who wath thlow to thtart, came in with a photo finish. She hath won Honorable Mention *and* ten dollarth *and* a pair of pinking shears *and* a box of Coath and Clarkth thread in evewy contheivable color. A round of applauth for Mith Moore! *(Class claps. Jane goes to get her prize. Mother Superior intercepts it beautifully.)*
MOTHER SUPERIOR. Not only am I thrilled with Miss Moore's prize, I am touched by her generosity. She has given the prize money to St. Mark's. The pinking shears she wants Miss McBride to have *(Miss McBride clutches them in saintly wonder to her bosom.)* and she wanted to split the thread with all of you, but I thought she should keep that for her very own. *(Mother Superior tucks the check in her pocket and hands the thread to Jane.)* Now

I hope all of you have a splendid vacation and that next year you'll all return to try for every kind of contest. This way we can prove over and over the superiority of our St. Mark's girls. (*Music as girls say goodbye to Miss McBride. Lots of chatter. Mother Superior exits along with class and Jane is left alone on stage with box of thread. She shrugs and laughs and music finishes.*)

END OF ACT I

ACT II

SCENE: *A school corridor. The second curtain is closed. September: Students returning. If taped music is used, students will make up conversation about what they've been doing. Last to enter, Jane and Mary who grab each other in joy.*

JANE. Golly, am I glad to see you. I thought you'd never get back. How was your summer?
MARY. Another round of tours. Did you get my cards from Switzerland and Italy?
JANE. Sure did. Did you get mine from Fox Lake?
MARY. Wish I'd been there.
JANE. Wish I'd been in Switzerland.
MARY. Listen, I've had enough hotel suites and dinner terraces to last me a life time. I missed you. Wait till you see what I found in Switzerland. It has given me theeee most marvelous, theeeeeee most wonderful idea. (*They exit. Mr. Goettinger enters carrying some instuments. He is a band leader. He has long arms and looks a bit like King Kong. Mother Superior enters.*)
MOTHER SUPERIOR. Ah Mr. Goettinger. I am delighted to see you. Are you prepared to give St. Mark's a winning band?
GOETTINGER. Of course, building a band is no problem provided you have some girls with talents and time for practice. In a few years you should have a first class band.
MOTHER SUPERIOR. YEARS! Dear Mr. Goettinger, I want a prize winning band next Spring. I have told the Mother's Club that if they provide the instruments and uniforms that we will win top prizes. You have a winning streak, anyway.
GOETTINGER. (*Flattered and embarrassed.*) Well, yes, my groups have placed first. Which contest have you in mind to win?
MOTHER SUPERIOR. Why the State Finals, of course!
GOETTINGER. Against St. Mary's and St. Luke's. They've been at it for years.
MOTHER SUPERIOR. Time to give them a run for their money.

(*As Mother Superior talks, bubbles start pouring in on them in great quantities.*) Why you have no idea what we can do when we put our minds to it.
GOETTINGER. But Mother . . .
MOTHER SUPERIOR. We mean to have a winning band by Spring and that is not a pipe dream.
GOETTINGER. I don't mean to burst your bubble, Mother, but . . .
MOTHER SUPERIOR. Speaking of bubbles, excuse me. I'll be right back. (*Mother Superior exits leaving Goettinger. He puts his head in his hands and begins to fight off the bubbles as he exits. Mother Superior re-enters.*) Tell that pair to come here. (*Jane and Mary enter. Mother Superior does not turn around. She gets up and walks back and forth with her back toward them. They get restless. Mother Superior whirls around and points her finger. Mary snaps to attention.*) Just look at you. Your first day back and look at you. Sophomores? No, babies. I am not sure I want either of you here at all. You're both a disgrace. I don't know what I'm going to do with you. What suggestions do you have? (*Silence.*) You're filled with ideas when it comes to trumping up something despicable. Which one of you filled all the sugar bowls with bubble bath? ANSWER ME!
MARY. It was my bubble bath.
JANE. I filled the bowls.
MARY. I had no idea it would bubble that much.
MOTHER SUPERIOR. What did you think would happen when hot water was poured on it?
MARY. I'm sorry.
MOTHER SUPERIOR. Mary Clancey. You and I simply do not see eye to eye. Sorry means one thing to you, another to me. Poor Sisters come home, try to have a peaceful moment and a cup of tea and what do they get, Bubbles. Soap bubbles. What are you going to do about it?
JANE. Get it out of the bowls. Right away.
MARY. Wash up the bowls right away.
MOTHER SUPERIOR. You can do better than that.
MARY. Wash all the dishes.
JANE. Wash everything.
MOTHER SUPERIOR. That's not even a good beginning. You

can make a daily list for me of all you've done each day. Then after a month, we'll talk again. Meanwhile, you are confined to your rooms and let me add this. One more misdemeanor and out you both go. On your way out, tell Sister Constance I want to see all girls who have musical instruments, or can play them—in the gymnasium at once. (*Jane and Mary exit* R. *Sister Angela comes in* R. *carrying huge, empty canvas.*)
SISTER ANGELA. (*To Mother Superior*) I'm forever blowing bubbles. Pretty little bubbles in the air.
MOTHER SUPERIOR. Now, Angela, don't get me started. I could absolutely kill them.
SISTER ANGELA. Why don't you? I would if you'd encourage me.
MOTHER SUPERIOR. You're a great one to talk. You let them cast poor Marvel Ann in plaster. It's a wonder she lived through it.
SISTER ANGELA. Where on earth did you hear such a thing?
MOTHER SUPERIOR. Well, as you've taught me, there is no such thing as a secret in this place. Listen, will you go get Mr. Goettinger and bring him to the gym. We're ready for the music auditions. (*Blackout. Curtain opens—Lights come up in gym. Mother Superior claps her hands and beckons in all the kids. They come with all kinds of brass instruments. Jane has a violin. Mary has a clarinet.*) We have a particularly good and gifted group of girls, Mr. Goettinger.
GOETTINGER. Of course, I can't guarantee anything, but I like a challenge. You say some of these young ladies are good musicians?
MOTHER SUPERIOR. I said they *will* be good musicians!
GOETTINGER. That girl with the violin. She has to go. (*Jane looks stricken.*)
MOTHER SUPERIOR. Why I don't see why she can't play her violin. She's the only one with a violin.
GOETTINGER. It's not possible, Mother. Bands consist of all wind instruments and percussion. But no strings.
MOTHER SUPERIOR. Bosh! Rules are made to be broken. (*Mary and Jane give her a look and she backs down quickly.*) What I mean, Mr. Goettinger, is that the world is starving for new concepts. If a band is good with all wind, wouldn't it be better with some strings?
GOETTINGER. She goes or I go.

MOTHER SUPERIOR. All right, Jane. We'll worry about your violin later. For the moment, you're dismissed.
GOETTINGER. *(Takes off his coat.)* All right. Let's audition. Have you got a cornet for me to hear? *(Florence Mackey stands up and blasts out taps. Goettinger studies. He signals her to the R.)* Let's go on. Do you have a clarinetist? *(Mother Superior grabs Mary and shoves her toward Mr. Goettinger. Mary begins but has too much saliva. She wipes her mouth on the back of her hand and starts again. Mr. Goettinger responds to the sound by gently putting his hands over his ears. Mother Superior, however, couldn't be more pleased. She exits. Mr. Goettinger lines up girls with instruments and points off stage R. They all exit. He remains standing. He takes out his music as they march out and bangs his baton. As he begins to lead the St. Mark's song the band is quite out of tune. The lights dim on them and come up on far L. Mary and Jane are squatting Indian style on benches. They are puffing away. The band continues to play and Goettinger continues to lead. Now the band is a bit better.)* [The Band can be pre-recorded, put on tape, and used this way if the KIDS can't play.]
MARY. *(Shouting at Jane over music.)* They are getting better.
JANE. They're lousy.
MARY. You're mad just 'cause Mr. Goettinger wouldn't let you play your magic violin.
JANE. It's his loss. You didn't manage to stay either and you play a wind instrument.
MARY. I wasn't disqualified. Mr. Goettinger says I'm tone deaf. He's quite wrong. I can play as well as any of them. Hey, I have the most marvelous idea. Something absolutely DEE-VINE!
JANE. What? Tell me instantly!
MARY. Do you think Mother Superior would let us go with the band as kind of official cheerleaders?
JANE. Frankly, no. Besides, who wants to cheer the losing team?
MARY. Mother is going to be furious if St. Mark's doesn't win and she is one lousy loser. I think it might be possible to guarantee our winning if we could be cheerleaders. I'm going to be a perfect student for a week and so are you and then we're going to get Sister Constance to ask her.
JANE. Constance isn't going to stick her neck out for us.
MARY. Yes she will. I'll work all week for her Missions. She'll do

it. I just know. (*Blackout. We hear the final phrase of* "Stars and Stripes Forever." *Second Curtain opens and we see 15 girls in a straight line of seats. They are at the band contest. Jane, Mary, and Kate are seated* C. *The bands are in the audience area.*) What do you think?

JANE. Most of the bands sound as bad as ours.

KATE. Except St. Mary's. They were really good.

MARY. They were? Were they good, Jane?

JANE. You heard them.

MARY. Yeah, but I'm completely deaf—remember?

JANE. Not deaf—just *tone* deaf. You can still hear music.

MARY. I don't think so. Not according to Mr. Goettinger.

JANE. Sh! (*Voice comes from back of theater, where the stage presumably is.*)

ANNOUNCER. Ladies and Gentlemen. The judges tell me their votes are tied so we are going to ask two bands to repeat "The Stars and Stripes Forever." The bands trying for the first prize are St. Mary's High School Band and the Band of St. Mark's Academy. (*Applause and screams.*) Begin please, St. Mark's. (*The band plays.* After the band number Mary goes through her pockets and produces three lemons and a knife.*)

JANE. What have you got?

MARY. Lemons.

JANE. What are you going to do with them?

MARY. When St. Mary's file on stage, get their attention and suck this lemon.

KATE. What will that do?

MARY. It will give them so much saliva they won't be able to blow.

JANE. How do you know?

MARY. I may be tone deaf, but I once played a mean clarinet, remember?

JANE. OK. I'll concentrate on the saxes.

MARY. Don't let the judges see you, Kate.

KATE. I'll get the trombones.

MARY. And I'll keep my eye on the clarinets. Watch that saliva start to flow!

ANNOUNCER. And now—St. Mary's High School Band. (*The*

* Band music and announcer's voice are on tape.

band starts and sounds good. Then, as the girls suck the lemons, there are many sour notes. They end to polite applause.)
MARY. How did they sound?
JANE. Sour—as sour as these lemons.
MARY. Serves 'em right. They were so darned sure of themselves.
ANNOUNCER. Ladies and Gentlemen, the judges' decision. First prize—$500 goes to St. Mark's Academy. (*Wild Applause. Mother Superior enters from* R.)
MOTHER SUPERIOR. See what hard work accomplishes? Come girls—let's congratulate Mr. Goettinger and the band. (*As the girls are leaving, Mother Superior stops Jane and Mary.*) May I see you two for a moment? The band director of St. Mary's has spoken to Mr. Goettinger about an incident that supposedly happened at the band concert. Do you two know anything about this incident?
JANE AND MARY. No, Mother.
MOTHER SUPERIOR. I must tell you that even though I have learned to distrust both of you, I have never felt that you were demoniacal. This incident, if it is true, is demoniacal. St. Mary's is accusing us of having used a salivary device to change the tonal structure of St. Mary's band.
MARY. (*Puzzled.*) A salivary device to change the tonal structure?
JANE. I don't understand.
MOTHER SUPERIOR. Supposedly some of our girls—unidentified —*sucked* lemons during St. Mary's performance rendering them unable to concentrate and play properly.
MARY. How terrible!
MOTHER SUPERIOR. You know nothing about this?
MARY. They're spoil sports. Their nose is out of joint.
JANE. They're just looking for excuses.
MOTHER SUPERIOR. I will admit that the evidence is very one-sided. I have checked Sister Constance and other St. Mark's girls, whom I trust explicitly, and I have found no one knows about this episode. What am I to believe?
MARY. They're just looking for a device that's face saving.
MOTHER SUPERIOR. All right. I will tell Mr. Goettinger to report back to St. Mary's with the news that after careful interrogation, I could find no such evidence to support their claim.

JANE. Absolutely.
MARY. When is the movie projector coming?
MOTHER SUPERIOR. The movie projector?
JANE. Yes, everyone said that if we won you were going to buy a movie projector.
MOTHER SUPERIOR. Yes, that *was* true. But now I have better plans for the money.
MARY. BETTER PLANS??
MOTHER SUPERIOR. Well, I'll tell you. There's a new home going up in this diocese for wayward girls. I think St. Mark's would make a real contribution if we gave them the prize money to spend on something important. Don't you think that's a good idea?
MARY. Wayward girls?
MOTHER SUPERIOR. Yes, and I would like you to make the announcement, Mary, at the next class meeting. In fact, you can go from class to class and make the announcement. Just tell them that the prize money will go to the new home for wayward girls.
JANE. That's terrible news to have to announce. So depressing.
MOTHER SUPERIOR. But you two were such good cheerleaders. You can cheer everyone up as you go along. (*Blackout. Jane and Mary, after Mother Superior exits, sing "Life With Mother Superior." This verse brings them up from sophomores to senior and as they march around with other girls, they seem to get more sophisticated and older looking. Tricks like pulling back hair on top of head is just one that can make a very nice change. During this, the benches from* D. C. *can be moved* U. *At the end of song they shout "Sophomore year, Junior year, Seniors at last."*)
JANE. *The Death of Abraham Lincoln.* What a Senior Class play. It should be a real winner. Who's in it?
RAMONA. Me. I'm Abe Lincoln.
JANE. Perfect. I'd know you anywhere. How do you like the idea that I am Herman, the field hand and I'm not popular with Miss Toomey or Sister Blanche.
MARY. You were the only one who volunteered to put burnt cork on your face.
JANE. That had nothing to do with it. I have a speaking part and you don't.
KATE. Which one?
JANE. Herman, the field hand. I'm in all three acts. Let's see . . . in the first act (*She thumbs through script.*), here it is, I say,

34

"Help, Help, please don't whip me." In Act II, I say, "Massuh, save me" and in Act III, I say, "We will never forget you, Abe Lincoln."
KATE. Wonderful. You can't even read them right. How are you ever going to say them right?
JANE. Do you have any lines?
KATE. No, I'm just dragged across the stage in Act III as a soldier.
JANE. (*To Ginger.*) What part did you get?
GINGER. A slave. Laurentis, and I say, "No" and "Save us all."
JANE. I don't envy Ramona with all her lines.
KATE. I wonder how they happened to pick her for Abe Lincoln.
MARY. 'Cause she's the tallest girl in the Senior Class and she has a beard. (*Sister Blanche enters.*)
SISTER BLANCHE. Miss Toomey will be right in. Do you all have your scripts?
ALL GIRLS. Yes, Sister.
SISTER BLANCHE. I had hoped St. Mark's would stage an operetta this year, but Miss Toomey feels your singing voices are not adequate. I do hope your speaking voices are. How many of you play male roles? Stand, please. (*One by one, all stand.*) You are all playing *male* roles? Oh, dear. (*At this point, Miss Toomey arrives.*) I'll leave you now with Miss Toomey.
GIRLS. Thank you, Sister. Good afternoon, Miss Toomey.
SISTER BLANCHE. (*Leaving.*) I'll drop in later to see how Abraham Lincoln's death is progressing. (*Exits R.*)
MISS TOOMEY. Bear in mind that this play—*The Death of Abraham Lincoln* shows what might have happened had Lincoln not been shot at Ford's Theater. (*3rd and 4th freshmen rush in to practice basketball.*) Please, girls, can't you see we're rehearsing? (*The girls tiptoe out.*) In Act I we see the poor Negro slaves working in the cotton fields and singing *My Old Kentucky Home* when Abraham Lincoln passes by. One of the field hands sees him and runs up to him and says, "Massuh, save me." Who has those lines? Who is Herman, the old field hand? (*Mary nudges Jane.*)
JANE. That's me. I say "Massuh, save me" and Peggy drags me away.
MISS TOOMEY. Ah, yes. Peggy is the slave owner. After you are dragged away, there is a touching scene with Lincoln vowing that some day all slaves will be free, etc. That gives you an idea of Act I. Turn to II, please. (*All thumb through scripts.*) P. 34—In

Act II we open with the slaves again—picking cotton. However, this time they are singing *Go Down Moses*. After they have sung one chorus, the slave owner—who's the Slave Owner?
PEGGY. That's me.
MISS TOOMEY. Oh yes, the slave owner, Peggy, enters and cracks her whip at the slaves.
JANE. *(Interrupting.)* That's when I say, "Help, help, please don't whip me."—and—and Peggy—
MISS TOOMEY. Yes—well we won't go into that now. The next scene shows Lincoln in his study, signing the Emancipation Proclamation and then we come to Act III. It opens with the conspirators plotting Lincoln's death. After that scene—which will be played in front of the curtain so we can change the set—we see the steps of the White House. The war is over and Lincoln is going out for a stroll. *(Ramona raises her hand.)* Yes, Ramona?
RAMONA. Pardon me, Miss Toomey, but why would I—I mean Lincoln—want a scroll? Did they use them?
MISS TOOMEY. I didn't say scroll, Ramona—I said "stroll." Lincoln is going out for a stroll—a walk.
RAMONA. Oh—thank you, Miss Toomey.
MISS TOOMEY. Now, where was I?
RAMONA. I was going out for a stroll.
MISS TOOMEY. Oh, yes. Now here is where the fictional part of the play develops. I think you will find that it is reminiscent of Shakespeare's *Julius Caesar*. The conspirators—That's Winifred and Lillian. *(Lillian raises her hand.)*
LILLIAN. But we're field hands.
MISS TOOMEY. Only in Act I. In Act III you change your costumes and makeup and you are conspirators.
LILLIAN. Oh—Thank you, Miss Toomey.
MISS TOOMEY. Now you conspirators are hidden in the crowd that has gathered to honor Lincoln. This is the climactic scene, of course, and because it is, we will rehearse this first today.
WINIFRED. What page, Miss Toomey?
MISS TOOMEY. It's on 109—Lincoln, stand C, please. Stand on that bench so we get the feel of height— *(They move bench to C.)* Now all the townspeople group around him. Let's see, that will be Florence, Oona Riley, Ramona Saplin, and Mary Clancey, Marie, Ann, Ginger, Kate. You group around the White House steps—

around the bench. The soldier with one arm—that's you, Florence—pretend you only have one arm (*The girls help her put it under her blouse.*) and stand here. The soldier with one leg—we'll give that part to you, Mary. Can you stand on one leg?
MARY. How's this?
MISS TOOMEY. Well, for a start, not too bad.
MARY. I'll use a big gun to lean on.
MISS TOOMEY. No, I think crutches would be better.
MARY. But they're poor people—they may not have—
MISS TOOMEY. (*Loudly.*) The other townspeople stand here and the conspirators group left, and watch intently. That's it. Now Lincoln— (*Ramona has been writing up on the bench.*) Lincoln! Ramona! (*She comes to.*) Your speech, please.
RAMONA. I'm sorry, I was trying to finish my chemistry. Which page, Miss Toomey?
MISS TOOMEY. P. 109.
RAMONA. Fourscore and seven years ago our fathers brought forth . . . (*Kate D., raises her hand.*)
MISS TOOMEY. What is it, Kate?
KATE. The war was still on when Lincoln delivered that speech.
MISS TOOMEY. Yes, I know, dear, but audiences love to hear the Gettysburg Address so we're substituting it for the speech in the original script. Go on, Ramona dear, I'm listening.
RAMONA. . . . on this continent a new nation conceived in liberty and dedicated to the proposition that all men are created equal. Now we are engaged in a great civil war . . . (*Kate's hand goes up again.*)
MISS TOOMEY. What is it, Kate?
KATE. According to my American History Book, the Gettysburg Address was delivered in Pennsylvania, not in Washington.
MISS TOOMEY. Haven't you ever heard of dramatic license? Keep going, Ramona. Louder, Ramona. (*Ramona's voice goes louder and higher.*)
RAMONA. . . . testing whether that nation or any nation so conceived and so dedicated can long endure. We are met on a great batttlefield of that war.
MISS TOOMEY. Lower your voice, dear.
RAMONA. We have come to dedicate a portion of that field as a final resting place for those who here gave their lives that that

nation might live. It is altogether fitting and proper that we should do this. But in a larger sense . . . (*Roger enters with hammer and nails and starts to repair something on stage.*)

MISS TOOMEY. Roger, I understood Mother Superior to say we could have the use of the auditorium today.

ROGER. Go right ahead—You're not in my way. (*He hammers some more.*)

RAMONA. We cannot dedicate, we cannot consecrate, we cannot hallow this ground. The brave men, living and dead, who struggled here, have consecrated it far above our poor power to add or detract. The world will little note nor long remember what we say here.

MISS TOOMEY. (*Over hammer noise.*) Louder, Ramona.

RAMONA. . . . but it can never forget what they did here. It is for us the living rather to be dedicated here to the unfinished work (*Sister Mary William enters with three girls.*) which they who fought here have thus far so nobly advanced. It is rather for us to be here dedicated to the great task remaining before us—that from these honored dead we take increased devotion to that cause for which they gave the last full measure of devotion—that we here highly resolve.

SISTER MARY WILLIAM. Excuse me, Miss Toomey, but the band left some instruments here. May we get them?

MISS TOOMEY. Well, tell them to take them quietly. I don't want to disturb Ramona. (*The girls cross and re-enter with a tuba, a cello, and a bass drum.*)

RAMONA. . . . that these dead shall not have died in vain—that this nation, under God, shall have a new birth of freedom— (*The hammering and hauling of instruments and the speech all end together.*) And that government of the people, by the people, and for the people, shall not perish from the earth.

MISS TOOMEY. (*Applauding.*) Cheers, everyone—applaud— Now Herman, the field hand—you burst through the crowd and say, "We will never forget you, Abe Lincoln."

JANE. We will never forget you, Abe Lincoln.

MISS TOOMEY. Now—as soon as Jane says her line, you three conspirators move in—say, "Sic semper tyrannis" and kill Lincoln.

WINIFRED. How? —With guns?

MISS TOOMEY. No—no—with your daggers. Each of you stab him in the back—just as Caesar was stabbed.

LILLIAN. She'll have to get off the bench, Miss Toomey. We can't reach her.

MISS TOOMEY. Ramona, dear—get off the bench so they can kill you. (*Ramona steps off bench.*) Now say your lines and KILL. Good. The crowd steps back—*step back!* Look horrified! Curtain! (*Nothing happens.*) Who is on curtain?

WINIFRED. Anna Marie Flaherty—but she's at band practice.

MISS TOOMEY. What is she doing at band practice? She should be here.

LILLIAN. Mr. Goettinger doesn't have another tuba player except Anna Marie Flaherty and they're practicing for the band concert.

MISS TOOMEY. All right—all right—someone pull it for now. Once more your line, Jane. Places!

JANE. We will never forget you, Abe Lincoln. (*The conspirators move in with "Sic semper tyrannis" and kill Ramona. The crowd steps back properly horrified.*)

MISS TOOMEY. Curtain— (*It jerks slowly—then opens.*) Fast—fast curtain! (*Ramona gets up and holds it closed.*) Oh why did I ever pick a tuba player for curtain girl? (*Blackout—music—lights come up on Jane sitting on a stool, back to audience as freshmen repair her make-up. They are at* R.)

FRESHMAN 1. Now hold still, Jane.

JANE. Ouch! You're killing me!

FRESHMAN 2. You shouldn't have eaten that candy. It's ruined your make-up.

JANE. But I didn't have any supper.

FRESHMAN 1. Neither did we.

JANE. You started making me up at 4:30!

FRESHMAN 2. Well! Someone had to be made up first.

JANE. Yeah, but this burnt cork itches and I've had it on for four hours.

FRESHMAN 1. Stop complaining.

FRESHMAN 2. Don't move.

JANE. I'd like to slip into the balcony and see the show.

FRESHMAN 2. We watched the first part from the wings.

JANE. How did it look?

FRESHMAN 2. Great!

FRESHMAN 1. Lincoln got a big hand.

JANE. She did!

FRESHMAN 2. Yeah! For her makeup. She looks just like Lincoln.
FRESHMAN 1. Only she doesn't sound like Lincoln.
FRESHMAN 2. No, she doesn't. Too bad she has to talk and ruin the effect. (*They work on Jane for a second in silence and then Sister Blanche enters.*)
SISTER BLANCHE. Has anyone seen Jane Moore? (*Jane gets up and turns and we see her burnt cork face.*) Jane Moore—get on the stage at once.
JANE. You mean they're up to my part?
SISTER BLANCHE. Not only are they up to it, but they've sung *My Old Kentucky Home* three times, waiting for you. (*Blackout. A platform with a curtain would be effective. Set it at an angle so we can see a small portion of the off stage area. The scenery could be a drape or a painted back drop. Benches on* R. *could be the seating area for the audience. The stage lights up. Chorus is singing "Weep No More My Lady." As they finish, all look to Miss Toomey, who is in the wings.*)
MISS TOOMEY. SING! (*As they start the chorus again, Jane and Sister Blanche arrive. We see Sister Blanche literally throw Jane on stage. When Jane recovers, she says:*)
JANE. We will never forget you, Abe Lincoln.
SISTER BLANCHE. (*In wings.*) That's your third act line.
MISS TOOMEY. Massuh, save me. Massuh, save me. (*But it's too late—the conspirators, 'tho they are dressed as field hands, move forward.*)
CONSPIRATORS. Sic Semper Tyrannis.
MISS TOOMEY. No—No. (*Lincoln falls, the crowd steps back horrified and the curtain closes fast.*)
SISTER BLANCHE. The performance has taken exactly 23 minutes.
MISS TOOMEY. 23 minutes for a three hour show.
MOTHER SUPERIOR. (*Bustling in from audience.*) That's the quickest death Lincoln ever had. What happened?
SISTER BLANCHE. Jane Moore said her third act lines instead of the first act ones.
MISS TOOMEY. What shall we do? Some of the cast hasn't even had a chance to appear on stage and they've rented costumes.
MOTHER SUPERIOR. You had better start all over again— But first let me talk to the audience. (*Mother Superior goes on stage—*

curtain opens—the cast frozen after their faux pas—stands in a frightened group as Mother Superior talks—Jane exits stealthily.) One of our actresses, in the fervor of her first major part, delivered her third act line instead of her first act one. We are certain you would not want to miss the next two acts, so we will proceed from just before the moment when Herman, the field hand, enters and speaks. *(The actors go into their positions and once more start "My Old Kentucky Home." Blackout. Second curtain closes. Three freshmen enter L. with play programs and pencils.)*

FRESHMAN 1. I got her autograph!

FRESHMAN 2. What did she write?

FRESHMAN 1. *(Reading.)* "Massuh, save me." And she signed it "Herman, the Field Hand."

FRESHMAN 2. She wrote: "We will never forget you, Miss Toomey," in my program.

FRESHMAN 1. Jane told me she might decide to be an actress— if she doesn't have to use burnt cork again.

FRESHMAN 2. They say she's been scrubbing for days and her face is still grayish. *(Sees Anna Marie.)* There's another Senior. *(Crossing to Anna Marie.)* Will you sign my program?

ANNA MARIE. *(Very pleased.)* OK. Any particular place?

FRESHMAN 2. Wait a minute. What part did you play?

ANNA MARIE. I pulled the curtain.

FRESHMAN 2. Oh— *(Grabs program.)* never mind— *(Three Freshmen exit R.)*

ANNA MARIE. *(Calling after them.)* What's wrong with curtain pulling?

JANE. Nothing. At least it saved you from putting burnt cork on your face with commencement a week away. I'm going to look like a full-blooded Seminole. *(These next are taped announcements. They can be accompanied by suitable pantomime and music. Sister Mary William enters with a stack of books. She becomes more bewildered as she hears the following announcement.)*

MOTHER SUPERIOR'S VOICE. Good morning, Sisters and girls. We will follow schedule 6 today and not schedule 3 as was previously announced. That means that period 2 and period 5 will interchange with period 4 and period 1. This will enable all Seniors and all band members to be free at period 7 for rehearsal

of Class Day ceremonies at period 8. Thank you. (*Sister Mary William exits with an "I give up" gesture.*)
A FEMALE VOICE (THE SEWING ROOM). Pardon this interruption, please. All Seniors are to go to the Sewing Room at once—to be fitted for their graduation dresses.
MISS TOOMEY'S VOICE. Will Lillian Quigley please come to the drama studio at once. Repeating—will Lillian Quigley please come to the drama studio at *once*. Bring your valedictory address, Lillian.
MR. GOETTINGER'S VOICE. All band members to the gymnasium now. Bring your instruments with you. (*Two band members enter—tuning up. Off mike.*) What is it, Mother? Oh yes. (*On mike.*) Mother Superior says wait until you get seated in the gymnasium before you tune up. Thank you. (*Band members exit.*)
MOTHER SUPERIOR'S VOICE. All seniors to the gymnasium at once. This is Commencement practice. Wear your heels please. (*A girl totters across the stage with very high heels.*)
SISTER BLANCHE. Mr. Goettinger—Mr. Goettinger—please remove your band instruments from the stage.
MOTHER SUPERIOR. Attention all Seniors. To the auditorium now for final Commencement instructions. (*Blackout. The second curtain opens. The lights come up. The class is in gowns. Each girl takes a cap and puts it on and Mother Superior goes to her platform.*) In a few minutes the guests will be arriving and I want to take this opportunity to give you your final instructions and to say my own personal goodbye to you. Under no circumstances today are you to look to the right or left of you. If the girl next to you faints, keep your eyes straight ahead. (*Ramona slumps.*) Ramona, stand up straight. You are not going to faint today. If the girl behind you falls off the platform, keep your eyes straight ahead. If the whole platform collapses, I want to find the entire Senior Class of beautiful women with their eyes straight ahead.
GIRLS. Yes, Mother.
MOTHER SUPERIOR. Now, there are going to be awards and prizes. And some surprises. Before you go out there. I want to tell you that Ramona won a fantastic scholarship to St. Brigit's College, Peggy Schlessman won one to Claremont. But what I am particularly proud of is that three of our Seniors are going to stay on at St. Mark's to follow religious vocations. That's a thrilling count.

(*Jane is cleaning her nails with her program, paying absolutely no attention to this discussion.*) Florence Mackey is one of them. Florence turned down two scholarships. Our second girl is Winifred Wertheim, State Tennis Champion and another of our top students, who will stay at St. Mark's. And the third one is a surprise to all of you. She is one of our most high spirited girls, Mary Clancey. (*Everyone applauds. Mary looks uncomfortable. Winifred and Florence look pleased. Jane has put her program down and she stares dumbfounded at Mother Superior.*) We have a few minutes before the band plays your entrance music. Perhaps you'd like to talk quietly among yourselves. (*The girls do. Jane eludes Mary. Mother Superior, grabbing Jane.*) Have you said anything to Mary?

JANE. I'm not interested in anyone that gets roped in.

MOTHER SUPERIOR. Jane Moore. You exasperate me. No one roped Mary in. She wants to stay. She's made it quite clear to me since Easter. Believe me, I did everything I could to talk her out of it.

JANE. I don't care about Florence or Peggy. They were dreary anyway, but whoever would have thought Mary would do it, somebody fun.

MOTHER SUPERIOR. She's not going to change just because she joins the convent.

JANE. Oh well, it doesn't matter.

MOTHER SUPERIOR. It most certainly does matter. It matters to Mary.

JANE. Let her do what she wants to do. If this is it—this is . . . it . . .

MOTHER SUPERIOR. You're going to do with your life precisely what you want to do. Why shouldn't Mary?

JANE. She's too young.

MOTHER SUPERIOR. Is Florence too young?

JANE. Florence was *never* young!

MOTHER SUPERIOR. Listen here, Jane Moore, I want a favor from you and I want it now. I think you owe me a big one. Since the only reason you graduated at all was compliments of one Mother Superior, tell Mary you're happy for her.

JANE. Oh all right. I'll tell her.

MOTHER SUPERIOR. But gently, Jane. Gently.

JANE. (*Wiping her eyes on her gown sleeve.*) O.K. O.K. But I will never understand, Mother. I will never understand.
MOTHER SUPERIOR. (*Giving her her hat.*) You will, Jane, you will. When you grow up. (*The March begins. They line up. Mother Superior walks to her platform and Jane begins to cross over to R. Mary enters from other side and crosses toward her. They pass each other by. Then they both turn and look at each other. They spend a second or so and then they both laugh. Jane grabs Mary and they hug. Their caps fall off and there is general confusion. Mother Superior sees them and follows closely behind. They begin to exit.*)
JANE. Why didn't you say anything?
MARY. I knew you'd think I was insane.
JANE. Well, what'll we do now? I'll have to work alone?
MARY. As a matter of fact, I just had THEEEEEEE most marvelous—— theeeeeeeeee most heavenly idea. (*She whispers in Jane's ear.*)
JANE. You're kidding. I don't believe you. You wouldn't. Sure I'll do it, but how?
MARY. Trust me.
JANE. Never again.
MOTHER SUPERIOR. (*Walks crisply by them.*) I wouldn't if I were you! (*Blackout. Finale with entire cast singing "Life With Mother Superior."*)

STAGING

"Life With Mother Superior" can be done with space staging. A second curtain is needed, as indicated in the script.

OTHER FURNISHINGS

3 benches—several stools
A railroad sign—"Willowood Station"
A small table and old fashioned dress form for the sewing room
An easel and small table for the art room

The fire escape is an enclosed, wooden chute with a door that can be pushed open from the inside.
For "The Death of Abraham Lincoln," a small platform with an attached practical curtain. Further directions in script.

PROPERTY LIST

16 sets dumbbells, painted bright colors
Gym whistle ⎫
Paperback   ⎪
Clarinet   ⎬ For Mary
Cigarettes ⎪
Tennis racket ⎭
4 suitcases: Jane, Mary, Winifred, Peggy
Violin—for Jane
Glasses—for Winifred
List of names and pencil—for Miss Connelly
2 oranges and 1 roll—for Kate
2 buckets
2 scrub brushes
Easel with painting on it
Paint brushes
Pinking shears—gold scissors
Wrist pincushion
Needles, thread—box of thread ⎫
Peach silk and pattern pieces ⎬ in shopping bags
2 prs. finished peach silk panties (Jane's)
Contest forms
Check
Plaster mask (plastic mask?)
Straws
Plaid dress material
Dress for sewing contest
Scripts—17 scripts, lettered—"Death of Abraham Lincoln"
Hammer and chisel
Makeup
Newspaper—for nun in robe
Stack of books
Long dark robe—for Mother Superior
Assorted musical instruments
2 band instruments
Bubble machine

Pitch pipe and baton—for Mr. Goettinger
Modeling clay
Plaster
Canvas
3—½ lemons and knife—for Mary
15 school hats—for girls
Stool and burnt cork—for 3rd and 4th freshmen
Burlap socks—for cotton pickers in "Death of Abraham Lincoln"
Pencils—for 1st and 2nd freshmen
Programs—for audience and for 1st and 2nd freshmen

COSTUME NOTES

The St. Mark's uniform is a green jumper. The blouse worn with it is an old fashioned, white middy with sailor collar, trimmed with green rick-rack. A green silk tie is worn with it. When the jumper is off, the girls are wearing full gym bloomers of green. Black cotton stockings and black gym shoes complete the outfit. The skirts should be about 10 inches from the floor. When the girls are at the band concert, they wear white sailor hats with green streamers.

Lillian and Florence wear wide red ribbons with "1st Honors" printed on them in gold lettering.

For commencement, each girl wears a white cap and gown.

For the Negro "make-up," try black cotton stockings over the face with eyes and mouth cut out.

The actors in "Death of Abraham Lincoln" wear bright colored flannel shirts over trousers and old felt hats. Lincoln wears a very false beard and frock coat and top hat. Mr. Goettinger wears a 1935 style suit.

LIFE WITH MOTHER SUPERIOR

WORDS: DION McGREGOR
MUSIC: MICHAEL BARR

Life with Mother Superior, nothing but nuns down on your knees

Life here couldn't be drearier, we're the unlucky ones grim little diocese
Life here ought to be cheerier

She gets less 'Norma Shearier' the more we pray
We have nothing to sing about and we confess

She gets more 'Wallace Beerier' day by day
We both have such a thing about Mother S.

Nobody ever gives her the slip she knows ev'ry move we make
Nobody told us what she was like or what life in stir would be

She never ever loses her grip she's getting to be a habit we
Somebody up there must be on strike or why does He never answer our

May never break 'tho' she's weirder and eerier
Pray'r to be free life with Mother Superior

She's yours and mine life with Mother Superior
Here in the pen she's a pain in the rearier

Too, too divine!
Wish we were men.

A——— men.
(Ah,——— men!)

NOTE: IN PERFORMANCE, MODULATE ½ A STEP FOR 2ND CHOS

THE EXERCISE SONG

Lyric by Dion McGregor
Music by Michael Barr

Ex-er-cis-ing stim-u-lates all the mov-ing parts and cal-is-then-ic-'ly cre-ates hap-py, health-y hearts. So, arms a-kim-bo, heads up high 'round and 'round the room we fly. Knees to chin, go one, two, three, hap-py, health-y you and me.

VAMP

OPTIONAL TAG

E, X, E, R, C, I, S, E, spells health, you see.

GIRLS AND FACULTY
(Singing and stumbling)

ALMA MATER

Dear St. Mark's, we pledge to you
Loyalty that's ever true
In our hearts forever share
Memories that flourished there.

Hail to thee, our Alma Mater
Hail to thee, our hallowed walls.
Gratefully we sing our praise
Gratefully we sing our praise.

(To be sung to melody of the traditional graduation song "Gaudeamus Igitur")

NEW PLAYS

★ **RABBIT HOLE by David Lindsay-Abaire.** Winner of the 2007 Pulitzer Prize. Becca and Howie Corbett have everything a couple could want until a life-shattering accident turns their world upside down. "An intensely emotional examination of grief, laced with wit." –*Variety.* "A transcendent and deeply affecting new play." –*Entertainment Weekly.* "Painstakingly beautiful." –*BackStage.* [2M, 3W] ISBN: 978-0-8222-2154-8

★ **DOUBT, A Parable by John Patrick Shanley.** Winner of the 2005 Pulitzer Prize and Tony Award. Sister Aloysius, a Bronx school principal, takes matters into her own hands when she suspects the young Father Flynn of improper relations with one of the male students. "All the elements come invigoratingly together like clockwork." –*Variety.* "Passionate, exquisite, important, engrossing." –*NY Newsday.* [1M, 3W] ISBN: 978-0-8222-2219-4

★ **THE PILLOWMAN by Martin McDonagh.** In an unnamed totalitarian state, an author of horrific children's stories discovers that someone has been making his stories come true. "A blindingly bright black comedy." –*NY Times.* "McDonagh's least forgiving, bravest play." –*Variety.* "Thoroughly startling and genuinely intimidating." –*Chicago Tribune.* [4M, 5 bit parts (2M, 1W, 1 boy, 1 girl)] ISBN: 978-0-8222-2100-5

★ **GREY GARDENS book by Doug Wright, music by Scott Frankel, lyrics by Michael Korie.** The hilarious and heartbreaking story of Big Edie and Little Edie Bouvier Beale, the eccentric aunt and cousin of Jacqueline Kennedy Onassis, once bright names on the social register who became East Hampton's most notorious recluses. "An experience no passionate theatergoer should miss." –*NY Times.* "A unique and unmissable musical." –*Rolling Stone.* [4M, 3W, 2 girls] ISBN: 978-0-8222-2181-4

★ **THE LITTLE DOG LAUGHED by Douglas Carter Beane.** Mitchell Green could make it big as the hot new leading man in Hollywood if Diane, his agent, could just keep him in the closet. "Devastatingly funny." –*NY Times.* "An out-and-out delight." –*NY Daily News.* "Full of wit and wisdom." –*NY Post.* [2M, 2W] ISBN: 978-0-8222-2226-2

★ **SHINING CITY by Conor McPherson.** A guilt-ridden man reaches out to a therapist after seeing the ghost of his recently deceased wife. "Haunting, inspired and glorious." –*NY Times.* "Simply breathtaking and astonishing." –*Time Out.* "A thoughtful, artful, absorbing new drama." –*Star-Ledger.* [3M, 1W] ISBN: 978-0-8222-2187-6

DRAMATISTS PLAY SERVICE, INC.
440 Park Avenue South, New York, NY 10016   212-683-8960   Fax 212-213-1539
postmaster@dramatists.com   www.dramatists.com